WOMEN IN BUSINESS DIGEST

WOMEN IN BUSINESS DIGEST

Foundational Considerations for (ERP) Enterprise Resource Planning

Galilee Digital Integrations: Marcia Thorne

AWS - Cloud Practitioner.
Associate in Science - Accounting Technology.
FSCJ
Graduate Accounting Degree Candidate.
Franklin University

❋ ❋ ❋

MARCIA THORNE

AUTHOR

Galilee Digital Integrations Firm :

Marcia Thorne

AWS - Cloud Practitioner.

Associate in Science - Accounting Technology.
FSCJ

Graduate Accounting Degree Candidate.
Franklin University

❋ ❋ ❋

BASIC ERP SYSTEM FUNCTIONS

The functional systems units work together through the Enterprise Resource Planning system architecture, where information is stored in databases and integrated through hardware, software, and middleware applications. Some modules relay real-time updates from other linked ERP systems forms that continuously provide updates as data is entered into the network ERP modules. Further information about business activities is accessible to authorized personnel by requesting the data from the organization's databases server (Motiwalla and Thompson, 2012).

❊ ❊ ❊

DATA ANALYSIS

The researcher conducted the study using a qualitative methodology examining primary and secondary sources. The author conducted topical searches to gather information using the Franklyn University library system, Google Scholar, accounting website links, and Google word searches to find scholarly journal articles and other writings on the topic. Used several additional resources to affirm the academic journal articles' findings from the topical searches using these different resources FASB, USDART, and our Motiwalla and Thompson Enterprise Systems for Management second edition publication.

For most of the articles reviewed, the authors used a qualitative approach for their study, followed by a few mixed methods techniques. After assessing and evaluating the information, it was organized into categories according to the relevant topic question heading and used in the discussion.

❋ ❋ ❋

DEDICATED TO

The Holy Spirit of Jesus who is my daily guide and constant companion because I embrace His vision as my personal life mission.

And to Mr. Jeff P. Jorgensen--Founder of "Blue Origin" which we dearly love and care about its continued, marketplace success weekly. Jeff, you are the love of my life daily! Comfort Peace, & Rest mean = We affirm each other in our daily life journey which we cultivate weekly, for Jesus, glory!

Then our habit of walking out our positive Vision together & seeing it come to full Completion is our custom. Just like having each other as Supportive & Encouraging Spouses is deliberate. Thank you, Jeff P, for helping me to finish my college degrees and for all the ways you poked, pushed, fostered, inspired, and encouraged me to keep writing and publishing my books.

It is my delightful pleasure to work alongside you in business and daily share your leadership life and "Blue Origin & its Space Marketplace Vision" as we are both enjoying watching more people participating with us in your "Millions of People Living & Working in Space" mission. Which did become our adventurous praiseworthy Life-Journey for the God of heaven's glory.

※ ※ ※

WOMEN IN BUSINESS DIGEST

FROM A FRIEND

"These broad arrays of initiatives which is only possible because a large team of talented people at every level are exercising their good judgement every day and asking, how can we make this Life better?" (Mr. Jeff P. Jorgensen) Daily...

❋ ❋ ❋

ABSTRACT

Trexin (2014) mentioned that "one of the most common issues with ERP implementations is that organizations do not sufficiently prepare for the undertaking." The project plans for enhancing the organization's functional capabilities long-term is significant for the management team to spend time discussing and finding the right technology to help the business realize its objectives is a topic for consideration.

Some ideas are presented from researching enterprise resource planning systems, examining the general areas of focus, time, passing information along, and things that could improve installation success—spotlighting the concerns surrounding the topics of risk to the project completion. This study will examine issues for mitigation as foundational to the system installation, including planning and strategy.

Also, what others have written and researched about finding pathways to success with the organizational ERP system integration. Management must plan for all the issues mentioned, as they directly impact the successful ERP implementation and the cost of owning and operating the system.

Keywords: Enterprise Resource Planning, communication, time sensitivity, total cost of implementation, project leaders, integration strategy, pre-planning, success ratio.

MARCIA THORNE

* * *

TABLE OF CONTENTS

1. Title

2. Author

3. Basic ERP System Functions

4. Data Analysis

5. Dedicated To

6. From a Friend

7. Abstract

8. Table of Contents

9. Foundational Considerations for Enterprise Resource Planning

10. The Purpose of the Research Discussion

11. We Examine the Purpose

12. Literature – Reviewing Other Writings

13. Noting the Role of Management in Systems Integration

14. The Need to make Governance Part of the Implementation

Methodology

15. Note Some Ethical, Operational, and Other Challenges that Management Faces

16. Addressing the Risk Factors that Affect Strategic Focus

17. Include ERP Architecture in the Discussion on Organizational Structure, Business Processes, and People

18. Watch for these Critical Success Factors in an ERP Implementation

19. Staying Time Sensitive to Ensure Strategic Project Focus is Maintained and Tested

20. Create a Team to Guide Change Management for the Useful Life of the ERP Implementation and System

21. Organize the Communication Needs and People-Related Risk through the Change Management Strategy

22. How do Pre-Planning Communication Channels Before and During an ERP Implementation Foster Success?

23. Communicating Clearly to Improve ERP Implementation Success Ratio

24. ERP Cost Considerations

25. Results

26. Summary

27. References

28. Accounting Code

FOUNDATIONAL CONSIDERATIONS FOR ENTERPRISE RESOURCE PLANNING

The general area to be discussed is considerations for enterprise resource planning. The focus will center around problems with communication and pre-project planning before and during a system installation. This study intends to highlight these areas because communication and planning are critical to achieving a successful ERP installation once the business vendor program has been selected.

Thus, the study will also explain the need to have several open communication channels, which is the most critical tool for moving the ERP system project plans forward and keeping it operating within budgeted time and costs. Lefran (2016) noted that "communication increases consistency for companies that succeed are those that have drafted effective business processes and rules."

More specifically, problems arise from inadequate pre-planning of communication channels that will be used for the ERP system project and how data and information are expected to pass along to the functional teams.

These problems are important for the business to consider because ensuring that adequate pre-planning and empowering communications are taking place among the teams is part of the foundational process. Which allows the teams to complete their particular job functions on the overall project without creating bottlenecks and work order delays.

As, information hoarding will prolong the ERP system implementation and increase the project costs because the teams will be forced to wait around, not knowing what to do next. These events could cause the budgeted resources to become exhausted or dry up during the project before its full completion.

Such events set up the environment for a loss on investment of the already spent funds, and system users may lose productivity morale reducing net profit output, thus significantly decreasing the business cash inflows and negatively affecting net income.

However, implementing enterprise resource planning systems can be a daunting task. Trexin (2014), mentioned that "one of the most common issues with ERP implementations is that organizations do not sufficiently prepare for the undertaking, recognize, or understand there are several key success factors to create a solid foundational strategy to reference throughout the effort."

We know several things about such problems from others who had successful ERP systems installed and the experience that taught them these lessons. First, an organization must factor this possible additional cost due to communication bottleneck into the project budget.

Because when pre-planning channels are not designated, information silos develop, which creates an environment where scope creep blurs the deliverables and extends the project cost and time. Project leaders are expected to communicate the importance of staying on task to each team as the consequences could not only stop the ERP system installation but also bankrupt the business.

Thus, drawing attention highlights the reason for streamlining the pre-planning and communication processes and using several systems for adequate consistency towards installation success. According to Cook (2013), "to communicate effectively, you need a communications plan. This should outline the central messages you want to convey to your workers and management and set out how you intend to communicate those messages."

Jesus commanded his followers in the Holy Bible to communicate clearly and to make long-term plans for events that have not taken place yet because it provides some control over unforeseen problematic issues. Such teachings are relevant principles for consideration in business and certainly during every phase of an ERP system installment.

Enterprise resource planning projects are considered major financial outlaying of cash and other business resources.

Recognizing the integrative role that communication and pre-planning can play in the overall outcomes at the project's starting point will improve timely, cost-saving decision-making processes, Motiwalla & Thompson (2012) mentioned. Finding relevant directional tips and consultive insights on how those two specific project components can foster more implementation success for organizations attempting to install a system is the reason for undertaking this research.

※ ※ ※

THE PURPOSE OF THE RESEARCH DISCUSSION

Is to examine what things are considered foundational and necessary to plan and implement an enterprise resource planning system. Somethings that increases the probability of success.

Next, identifying factors that could hinder the elements of success.

Then discussing both aspects in an informative way to educate readers and decisions makers on enterprise resource planning considerations because most businesses could benefit from gaining additional tips on this subject area. If they have or are thinking about installing or upgrading an existing ERP system to improve their operations, net income, and reporting speed from customizing reports to make quicker real-time business decisions. Keeping in context that pre-planning is done for meeting the established organizational objectives and using several communication channels will help the project deliverable milestones to stay focused on achieving time and budget allotted constraints.

This article by Cook (2013) hinted that "as a first approximation, you can't communicate too much on an ERP project. Yet communication, while important, isn't part of the core functions of implementing ERP. As such, it is often skimped or overlooked entirely."

WE EXAMINE THE PURPOSE

This study aims to find foundational elements needed in enterprise resource planning projects. Then highlight such factors the software industry considers critical to integrate during project implementation that will increase the completion of the installation with a favorable outcome.

The research discussion question is "Foundational Considerations for Enterprise Resource Planning?"

The following two questions will be considered for this study.

1) What role does strategic focus and time contribute to creating a successful ERP implementation environment for the organization?

2) How do pre-planning communication channel and system use before and during an ERP implementation foster success?

* * *

LITERATURE - REVIEWING OTHER WRITINGS

What role does strategic focus and time contribute to creating a successful ERP implementation environment for the organization?

Caldwell (2020) highlighted that "An ERP implementation typically is broken down into six primary stages, or phases, spread over months, or years. The process needs to begin well before a decision about which product to buy and continues after initial rollout of the system."

✻ ✻ ✻

NOTING THE ROLE OF MANAGEMENT IN SYSTEMS INTEGRATION

The company's board of directors and upper-level management are to work with the IT management teams, which should include a systems analyst and project manager, and the ERP system vendor during each of the seven-system development life cycle phases.

This is done to ensure the new ERP system transition is as smooth as possible. The system does what the company envisioned it doing during live operation before approving a project that will increase the risk to the enterprise assets or hinder meeting the company's objectives and negatively affecting net profits.

Preston (2022) noted that "project managers and system analysts can leverage software development life cycles to outline, design, develop, test, and eventually deploy information systems or software products with greater regularity, efficiency, and overall quality."

The end goal is to improve the customer satisfaction experience with the deliverables and enable users to perform their jobs efficiently.

❖ ❖ ❖

THE NEED TO MAKE GOVERNANCE PART OF THE IMPLEMENTATION METHODOLOGY

Governance is the written guidelines that will be followed throughout the project. After the ERP system implementation, these documents guide the long-term roles, functional responsibilities, and accountability measures the organizational system owners are to follow. The merit of governance is to define roles and procedural mandates in a detailed understandable procedure manual format.

That elaborates on what makes up the ERP system, the organizational objectives that the system will address, and the people and job functions to support the guidelines outlined in the system governance, Motiwalla, and Thompson (2012). Amazon's (AWS) OpenSearch service offers 'security information and event management, with application and infrastructure monitoring.' TekStream stated that "database platforms, middleware engines, and ERP and CRM systems make up the backbone of a business."

Implementing an ERP system is a critical path in the project. Even after testing the components, processes, integrative applications, users, and written guidelines, underlining issues will only surface when the system is live.

During the system design process, an implementation strategy is selected based on the project's organizational needs, costs, and time frame. The business may choose a vanilla strategy that requires no changes to the ERP system application modules. However, the company processes must change to fit into the ERP system functional modules.

The following customization method will involve customizing the ERP system. Sometimes preexisting processes are re-engineered or middleware applications installed to make all the programs communicate and work together with advantages and disadvantages. Any changes to an organization's business processes require proper planning and testing in a development environment of every application that will integrate with the live system (Motiwalla and Thompson, 2012).

The merit is to create the best possible environment for successful implementation because that will make a satisfied customer. The company could then start accessing the cost-saving benefits of the ERP system to meet its business objectives.

In addition, Panorama Consulting Group (2021) explained that 'ERP project governance is critical to ensuring your effort stays on track, from the initial planning stages to well past your go-live date. This governance is maintained by a core group of influencers that direct the implementation.' Using a functional team to drive the governance and implementation of ERP system applications is a critical process that requires a lot of resources for an extended period.

❋ ❋ ❋

NOTE SOME ETHICAL, OPERATIONAL, AND OTHER CHALLENGES THAT MANAGEMENT FACES

Management could face issues about the company's ethical culture because during organizational functional changes; the lower-level managers will be more concerned with the things that affect their departments' production numbers or performance bonuses caused by the new system.

Sharing certain information may cause dysfunctional behaviors, management should have a plan to mitigate and address such issues. Then the operational challenges faced by the vendors who require sensative company data for testing soundness of the informational output before live data sampling using the new system.

The ERP implementation teams will all be responsible

but under management risk reduction watchful plan. As the type of information access needed according to the industry standarderds for best information technology pratices must be based on the team role for the specific project which will be different.

Management needs to plan how much and the kind of information they make available to external entities on the new system.

Security of the system users and securing the new ERP system from the users will be an ongoing issue to protect the integrity of information from many categories of risk. Training all system users will be essential to help decrease avoidable challenges like password compromises or too much non-job-related cross-functional access.

Consider these pratices as cost-saving benefits of the new ERP system because data output errors are costly to fix (Motiwalla & Thompson, 2012).

ADDRESSING THE RISK FACTORS THAT AFFECT STRATEGIC FOCUS

The planning team must find the ERP system risk factors that will hinder a successful installment and mitigating them increases the ratio of completing the installation. Because when business functional operating processes are changed, it increases completion risk and exposes the entire project to delay or failure.

Keeping a keen eye on possible dangers to the ERP implementation will help maintain the project's overall strategic focus. Management should consider having written guidelines to navigate potential issues by formulating a plan to address project risk concerns, thus decreasing installation failure, and fostering clear communication about deliverables and time requirements.

Performing an in-depth organizational needs analysis and applying the results to the vendor selection is a foundational ERP installation step. Fostering a risk-sensitive culture to apply management risk mitigations controls will increase the selection of a sutiable system and create a favorable vendor system selection that will match the business objectives needs Wright & Wright, (2002) discussed. To ensure a successful enterprise resource planning (ERP) system installation.

Managing time is foundational to achieving strategic objectives and focus for the organization, and addressing risk is the starting point. In implementing enterprise resource planning systems, organizational performance and the implementation duration are significant factors that impact strategic focus and increase anxiety concerning crucial performance indicator measurements (Anderson et al. 2011).

The organization must consider risk factors that can affect its strategic focus before and during the installation and according to Chofreh et al (2018) such measures must consider taking sustainable steps for long-term system usage. Areas for risk considerations during the preplanning phase are ERP functions which are system management concepts, then the possible organizational impact from the automation of tasks.

Evaluating unit of production performance elements is another area where management can expect issues to develop before and during the ERP implementation project. Due to the new changes in how the code was written for the data integration to process departmental contribution to net income and the altered process configurations for determining expected benchmarks from the new information flow and evaluational changes (Jacobs & Bendoly, 2003).

❋ ❋ ❋

INCLUDE ERP ARCHITECTURE IN THE DISCUSSION ON ORGANIZATIONAL STRUCTURE, BUSINESS PROCESSES, AND PEOPLE

An article from Florida Tech (2022) highlighted that "ERP systems are designed to facilitate sharing of information across functions to eliminate inconsistency and duplication of effort and when selecting a platform. The organization should consider the various ERP modules which align with their strategic, economic, and technical goals." The business could use the 'system-development life cycle processes (SDLC)' to help with such decisions.

It starts by performing an analysis that talks with and gathers information from system users. Radack (2009) noted "the five phases of the system development life cycle (SDLC) process. Developing, implementing, and retiring information systems from initiation, analysis, design, implementation, and maintenance to disposal and benefits of integrating security into each phase of the system development life cycle."

The fundamental objective for management to address when thinking, discussing, or planning to make any changes or implement a change to its structure, business processes, and procedures the change leaders must consult with and open lines of communication between people.

The changes will have an impact on workers, customers, and all system users making it foundational for management to guide the conversation in the direction of meeting the business objectives by involving users. Because the input from users will be critical to ensure the project's success.

Akbulut & Motwani (2005) noted, "the road to ERP success is gaining an understanding of the End-User perceptions." Meaning prior discussions must take place to gather information from the current system users who will be affected by the proposed changes.

Those users' voices are critical to help with system design and crafting the integration architecture because users are the ones who have to perform their job functions with the new system and meet expected production outputs.

Management needs to learn from the present system users what problems they are experiencing with the current system; this way, the new system or the upgrades will not repeat the functional difficulties found in the architecture that the users may be experiencing.

When changes are in the planning phase this is the best time to incorporate different processes that alleviate frustrations to increase efficiencies and maximize the return-on-investment benefits to the organization. However, at the end of the day. The primary goal of implementing changes is to meet the company's goals and objectives.

It is achievable through the workers' ability to perform their jobs with tools that efficiently increase net profit production output. But iterative input from system users is essential for the implementation to meet its ROI. According to Panoroma Consulting Group (2012), "the best way to ensure new software is being utilized properly is to train employees and develop and implement a communications plan as part of the company's organizational change management activities."

WATCH FOR THESE CRITICAL SUCCESS FACTORS IN AN ERP IMPLEMENTATION

Critical success factors in a successful ERP implementation are—Project startup planning, project scope, project management teams for functional and technical areas, change management plan for the implementation, and managing the project cost.

Trexin (2014) mention the organization should "consider the goals, requirements, processes involved in creating a foundational ERP strategy from which project leaders may draw actionable first steps. Preparing all necessary information, communicating, appropriate personnel, and receiving management buy-in before the work even begins."

1) Project startup plannings are the procedures and processes to examine the written guidelines for coordinating the different people and additional policies that leaders, vendors, and teams must follow in each wave of the ERP implementation towards meeting the project goals in a set time frame.

Consider them critical factors essential to success because

many prior decisions regarding the ERP system will go through the final checks and review process to move forward with the system implementation by getting it off the ground after the vendor and software product selection.

At this point in the project the ERP system owners set, the tone-at-the-top and provide additional resources, including their oversight, time, and directional input. The users-buy-in come through a commitment to job changes, training, and not trying to work around the new functional procedures.

Together they form the resources and organizational change processes commitment needed to support the project from start to finish, Motiwalla & Thompson (2012) highlighted.

2) Project scope, "What's Included?" it's the agreed-upon deliverable 'what the customer gets' from the vendor and implementation team with the ERP system; think of it as the line-item contract details for the work order.

The project scope is a critical success document for the implementation because it lists the components included in the project fees. Like the work order time frames, milestones, and percentages of the ERP system installation completion progress at specific points, and precisely the things projected for completion on each specified date--till all the project parts are delivered and accepted by the owners.

Trexin (2014) states, "focus on critical business use cases, how users will work within those processes to define scope. Align and prioritize with the organization, deliver the implementation 85-90% to immediate derive benefits drive towards those initial benefits."

3) A critical part necessary for installation success is the project management teams for functional and technical areas because ERP system implementation relies on several groups

of individuals. With different skill sets and knowledge levels, who will work together using the project scope and installation model. Install, test, monitor the system, and train the user groups.

Teams coordinate and communicate continuously, thus ensuring the correct type of progressive actions are taking place to meet the scope milestones on time Motiwalla & Thompson (2012) discussed.

Trexin (2014) mentioned, "defining responsibilities the project team being composed of full-time personnel, project managers, others representing core business areas and IT. A cohesive working relationship with the consultants, subject matter expertise when necessary to make important project-focused decisions."

4) Creating a written real-time working change management plan for the implementation is another critical pathway component for success with the ERP system installation goal map. In context, it means thinking of the 'worst-case scenarios' and planning to address such issues before they arise.

The normal is to plan for everyone on board and participating in the change process because it is suitable for attaining the organization's objectives. However, individuals have personal concerns and fears that may not be rational but still need addressing through the change management system.

Thus, providing many avenues for the affected and other users to communicate and receive timely, reliable information will keep nasty rumors at bay. To include a way for affected users to share anonymously with the Human Resource department.

Furthermore, engaging the users with different educational and relevant training delivery systems modalities will benefit the company during and after the installation process (Motiwalla & Thompson, 2012).

5) A critical element is Managing the Project Cost; this is

an essential component in the ERP system implementation because cost over-runs could prevent the project from completion and the system from being fully installed.

Trexin (2014) suggested creating "a realistic budget to include all costs for the implementation, such as software, hardware, and staff resources as most organizations will expect a timely ROI from an ERP project a projected profitability date."

There are many models of installation structures that an organization can use, and some of them may be cost-effective short term but turn out to be more expensive to maintain or expand later. These issues are part of the project cost that factors into the total cost of the ERP system ownership. System changes during and after installation could quickly get out of control from project scope creep requests, which change requirements and cause completion delays.

Making the ability of the project manager's leadership a critical decision element to reach goals on time Motiwalla & Thompson (2012) emphasized.

✷ ✷ ✷

STAYING TIME SENSITIVE TO ENSURE STRATEGIC PROJECT FOCUS IS MAINTAINED AND TESTED

According to Oliver & Romm (2002), strategy, focus, time, and testing such risk factors need a customizable written plan to ensure that the different teams understand the procedures they are to follow during unfavorable events that may slow down or stop the project. Strategic focus incorporates the values driving the ERP system adoption by the organization and which spheres of ERP implementation models they decided to use. Adhering to the time frame mandate reduces critical project pathways stress from unnecessary risk exposure. Maintaining focus fosters better decision-making input and increases data accuracy throughout the implementation teams, increasing success ratios, as their impact will flow through the entire system project.

Foundational to such an undertaking higlights a requirement that management must make resource provisions for the businesses' long-term needs. Ensuring they address the correct business requirements objectives with the ERP system modules when planning their strategic timeline for its completion is imperative.

Allen (2008) mentioned that it would be in the best interest of the organization to use data tools when testing their system controls.

The business's long-term vision remains a central time-sensitive strategic focus to overcome the risk complexities in such projects. Companies have formulated strategic goals to affirm their reasons for adopting the usage of an ERP system. Note that entire organizations usually experience reshaping using this type of information technology application (Oliver & Romm, 2002).

Because every team has a time-sensitive task to perform, everyone must maintain a time sensitivity awareness towards the project elements, which are foundational to maximizing the usage of allotted resources. Understand that risk problems can change the strategic project focus. They arise from improper planning and breakdown in communication among teams making them relevant and vital to consider and address. Risk management is foundational for increasing chances of producing a favorable outcome with the ERP system installation, which are known to be high-risk projects Beheshti & Beheshti (2010) discussed.

Teams must plan enough time to evaluate their implementation strategy and ongoing progress. Data output accuracy is a high-risk testing factor during implementation, making it a critical pathway problem requiring close attention. The process of testing and having good data keep the project integration moving forward to completion and lowers data corruption risk, saving process reworking costs and strategic time.

The area of system testing is foundational and has a lot of cause for concern because risk increases during system testing to meet strategic objectives. Every opportunity to keep a project focused and on time is relevant to staying within the required timetable for project completion, conducting many functional tests during integration on the ERP system, and evaluating the data output is critical to meeting the project's strategic objective. That must pass those pre-set integration criteria, and efficiency ranges benchmarks.

The installment teams must stay ahead and maintain a working knowledge of which information samples demonstrate functional efficiencies of effective system integration and adjust accordingly.

Accurate data output is foundational to delivering the ERP system to the organization and critical to proving the system's reliability before it can go live in production. Management has to plan for continued business production operations and function within established budget constraints as organizations use their enterprise resource planning systems to focus on operations and customers (Beheshti & Beheshti, 2010).

CREATE A TEAM TO GUIDE CHANGE MANAGEMENT FOR THE USEFUL LIFE OF THE ERP IMPLEMENTATION AND SYSTEM

Change Management takes on one of the essential roles when an enterprise resource planning system is to be implemented at an organization to coordinate its business processes for achieving objectives.

Change Management does not start with the implementation of the ERP system. Still, it is part of the foundation in the planning phase, and it continues throughout each step of the integration to when the vendor help desk is set up for continued system support and beyond. Business processes are continuously being tweaked to ensure proper system functioning.

Ultra-Consultants (accessed 2022) noted that "as a first strategy, it is key to articulate the case for change clearly. As the ERP project gets underway, we encourage teams to communicate project scope, rollout strategy, and implementation schedule." Making the role of Change Management a vital part of every phase of integrating the ERP system.

The people who will be involved in the Change Management process for the organization will have to work closely with the system analysis team and the vendors on the application, customizing the software or reengineering processes to fit the applications. Gaining end-user input for functionality and providing system training to get buy-in for the employee job function changes or job tasks realignment.

Miller (2020) stated that "organizational change refers broadly to the action's businesses take to change or adjust significant components of its organization. This may include company culture, internal processes, underlying technology, infrastructure, corporate hierarchy, or another critical aspect and can be adaptive or transformational."

Change Management teamwork fosters an environment where the organization's upper management involvement remains visible and active, and the enterprise resource planning implementation remains a priority.

✻ ✻ ✻

ORGANIZE THE COMMUNICATION NEEDS AND PEOPLE-RELATED RISKS THROUGH THE CHANGE MANAGEMENT STRATEGY

The organization management team's communication to the employees through multiple mediums is a critical area often overlooked when incorporating input for a new or redesigned enterprise resource planning system for implementation.

Communication does not have an end date because

ERP system tasks are ongoing into the future, creating the never-ending job of communicating or reminding employees of its purpose. Such discussions serve as enterprise risk management reinforcements that address why the company should use an ERP system's capabilities among the upper management team to mitigate and track risk exposures.

Iterations between middle and lower levels functional management teams to address the employees' fears and job task adjustment concerns get lost among the noise of installing an ERP application. Communication with employees usually decreases during this type of project.

According to Prabhakaran (2022), "organizations need to communicate the 'why' behind the change to your employees, so they understand the requirements for the change; when your employees buy into the need for the change, they will become fully involved in related activities."

Highlighting those iterations among the management teams and the employees remain a critical part of the ERP system planning, implementation, and practical usage process.

However, to address the people-related issues that usually arise, the organization's communication channels must be open enough for employees to voice job changes or other employment-related concerns. Thinking long-term beyond the immediate ERP installation, Management must promptly provide feedback or answers to clarify the employees' thinking about such issues.

Management must give urgent attention to this critical area because the employees will have to make many flexible ongoing adjustments that could take years. This requires the HR department and department managers to provide a unique channel for employee engagement and organizational objectives reeducation to show employees where they fit into the new or redesigned business processes.

Management's proactive communication can put many employees' fears to rest, thus reducing barriers to organizational change (Motiwalla & Thompson, 2012).

Stobierski (2020) highlighted that **"Transformational changes** have a larger scale and scope than adaptive changes. They can often involve a simultaneous shift in mission and strategy, company or team structure, people and organizational performance, or business processes."

The management representatives are expected to be very informative and clear when communicating about the ERP system adaption process. It is necessary to show employees how their job functions, titles, and tasks will relate to helping the organization attain its objectives and short term goals. Next, creating a feeling of belonging for the employees to keep making idea contributions to the organization will foster the type of dynamic behaviors necessary for the system implementation success.

Underline this point on your list of foundational principles to achieving a productive functional environment for the enterprise resource planning system to function. Because a company must allow their employees to see themselves as part of the whole this can only be done by effective multimodal, iterative communication (Motiwalla & Thompson, 2012).

Employees will usually remain active participants in the organization's change program when they feel a sense of belonging beyond their end-user input for the system development process that was conducted during the ERP planning sessions.

※ ※ ※

HOW DO PRE-PLANNING COMMUNICATION CHANNELS BEFORE AND DURING AN ERP IMPLEMENTATION FOSTER SUCCESS?

Potts (2020) discussed the importance as "Starting by communicating sooner than later because delay can become dangerous and needs to be managed carefully; redundancy is not bad, consider varied mediums; communicate early and often, even at the very early ERP stages of transformation."

Continuous communication, addressing and mitigating risk, and staying time sensitive because these things have a direct effect on cost and total cost of owning the ERP system such considerations were proven as foundational requirements among the teams. Pre-planning the communication channels and developing a written, tested plan for outbound and inbound iterative exchanges will improve the success ratio for the ERP project.

Management must determine the frequency of making information available to employees and functional teams to ensure the project stays on budget and on time to maximize allocated resources. It is foundational to prevent teams from waiting on information to do their part of the project. When people know where to get clarity with project questions or get someone to inspect their completed work so they can move on to the subsequent implementation phase, it fosters an environment where the team members are empowered to keep the project moving forward on schedule.

Thus, the reason for having multiple communication channels where decision-making data can flow quickly is for real-time updates that will allow continued system production progress. Finding and implementing a method that creates the best possibility of completing a successful installation decreases overall project cost over time and enhances the Enterprise resource planning system's useful life.

Management's ability to make cost-saving informed decisions regarding beneficial choices for the organization is attainable through meaningful communication of data and timely relevant information flowing through many channels (Mabert et al., 2003)

※ ※ ※

COMMUNICATING CLEARLY TO IMPROVE ERP IMPLEMENTATION SUCCESS RATIO

The project team leaders must maintain clarity when communicating information and provide data to convey and achieve effective knowledge transfer to the organization; this is a foundational requirement. Information travels through the usual channels from the implementation teams to the people that own the Enterprise Resource Planning system and those responsible for the system operations as it goes into production.

Using a wide range of communication systems and devices will increase; the level of understanding and working knowledge throughout each phase of the project installation, thus lowering and mitigating risk factors and keeping the business objectives moving forward towards timely completion (Wang et al. 2007).

One crucial consideration is looking at some failed ERP system implementations, which is using another mode of communication to increase the possibilities of having a successful ERP experience. Giving thought to what did not work helps clarify the management decision-making understanding of what will work for the organization.

This author highlighted the need for pre-implementation education of management, Momoh et al. (2010). As a foundational part of things to incorporate into planning for an ERP installation and change management educational topics.

Using reliable data increases the organization's success probability and maintains strategic project focus. It will help leaders make informed and better decisions before, during, and after they understand the unique risk associated with implementing enterprise resource planning systems.

Such risks are considered in the project planning phase. The plans are often referred to and updated as needed during the ERP installation phase as a form of communication with the system owners and functional teams. Implementation challenges will arise as uncontrollable events are likely to occur. Adjustments for such changes must happen through the established iterative process; available through the specified communication methods because getting timely decision-making information to others is considered a high priority to avoid extending the project time (Wang et al. 2007).

Addressing the total cost of the ERP system ownership needs and how it relates back to creating a return benefit to the organization will require performing a financial needs analysis to determine the percentages of return on investment. Effective communication must happen among the teams and management to ensure the project remains adequately funded and progresses till completion.

Managers' lack of participation in the enterprise resource preplanning phases could slow down an installation because management or business units may not fully understand how communicating their particular requirements during preplanning could improve their departments' net output.

Also, managers may not contribute fully to performing a thorough evaluation of the operating processes in their respective departments to contribute to accurate technology resource needs for the organization's planning allocations. Units may fail to effectively evaluate any operational or other bugs in the current system that they are experiencing; these are reasons for management and the project planning team to ensure communication about the reason for the company's ERP system is straightforward and often.

Such issues are common organizational risks and could decrease with continuous communication and education to management and staff on the company's short-term and long-term growth projection needs to maintain and gain industry market share and how the enterprise resource planning system modules are being designed to help everyone work together to achieve these objectives (AboAbdo et al., 2019).

ERP COST CONSIDERATIONS

Cost is a foundational consideration reflected in two forms; the first is the total ending implementation cost, and the second is the ongoing cost of owning the ERP system. To ensure they remain strategically focused on meeting their task on schedule and keep the project progressing to completion. Management has to consider the functional and technical limits and capabilities of the proposed ERP system, what the organization is seeking to improve from the investment and their expectations of the information technology system adoption.

A successful ERP system implementation is achieved through thoughtful pre-planning to alleviate unnecessary pressure on the teams. All these factors affect implementation strategy choices, which reflects later in the amount of time used on the total project, the installation realized cost, and the implications it will have on the organization's total cost of ownership (Stratman, 2007).

Management considers the challenges of planning its available resources and how project resources are impacted to ensure the ERP implementation does not run out of funding or personnel. The project manager recognizes that the specific differences in implementation approaches have a price tag. These are foundational to choosing the suitable ERP system implementation methods on the market because prices vary and time to implement has a cost attached. However, performing modifications to the ERP modules could increase installation costs if they were not factored into the initial system cost during preplanning.

Accounting code topics relevant to this study are 360 equipment, 350 intangibles, 320 investments if system financing is involved, 805 business combinations for integrating other units on the ERP system, and 410 for the legacy system asset retirement (FASB).

The total cost of ownership for the ERP system involves all the prices the organization will incur for some time because they elected to purchase the system. Upfront and long-term costs of owning the system depend most on the architecture design of the integrating modules, processes, third-party additions, staffing requirements, and customizations.

Such fee includes the initial upfront cash outlays for planning, consulting, personnel doing additional functions, system implementation, training, updates, customizations, functional down times for installation, maintenance, and other skilled staff.

Suppose the system is cloud-based or premises-based; the useful system life and possible increased utility bills from operating the ERP system are associated costs. These expenses are fractured into the total cost of ownership when considering and comparing upfront and ongoing total cost of owning the system cash requirements.

Many costs are associated with buying and owning a particular Enterprise Resource Planning system. However, these expenditures can be flexible because there are many system options to choose from, and ERP systems are expandable, meaning as the organization grows, its integrative technology resources can grow or downgrade. Having such options available significantly lowers the upfront cost for businesses to acquire more functional technology to maximize their available resources and reduce operational costs, Motiwalla & Thompson (2012) highlighted.

RESULTS

The discussion's primary focus is to uncover foundational considerations for enterprise resource planning, which centers around how organizations arrive at their conclusion when formulating technology integration plans for adoption. Enterprise resource planning systems had been thought of as having the ability, when implemented, to change the entire organization for good.

Still, the study found that many risk factors develop and need addressing throughout the process. From the role, users will occupy with new technology applications, Oliver & Romm (2002). Key findings were discussed that answered the research questions that were central elements of productivity to keep the ERP system installation moving forward in an organization.

Greater detail was discussed in focusing on the business strategy and uncovered evidence to highlight the critical topics management needs to address. Before, during, and after they decide on a vendor's product to meet the business cost and efficiency change objectives which are the main reason for using an enterprise resource planning system.

Maintaining an environment that fosters cost-saving process integrations of operations requires pre-planning functional strategy and ensuring time management has accountability measurements that align with the overall organizational system practical productivity (Beheshti &

Beheshti, 2010).

The key project and team leaders are reminded that when communicating information, they must use multiple mediums to reach different audiences and provide the data to convey effective knowledge transfer for functional usage of the explanations throughout the organization. Including the people that own the ERP system and those individuals responsible for the system operations as it goes into production (Wang et al. 2007).

※ ※ ※

SUMMARY

The significance of using the right implementation approach during the ERP system installation weighs on the allocated time for the project to start and end. The selected strategy must accommodate budget mandates because it provides the needed time for the organization to redesign its processes to increase the business's performance capabilities.

However, the accelerated method of ERP implementation delivered more benefits upfront but is not practical for every project, Anderson et al. (2011). Continuous communication, addressing and mitigating risk, and staying time sensitive these things have a direct effect on cost and total cost of owning the ERP system. Thus, such considerations are foundational requirements for pre-planning an ERP installment project.

Finding and implementing a method that creates the best possibility of completing a successful project decreases overall project cost over time and enhances the ERP system's useful life.

Management's ability to make cost-saving informed decisions regarding beneficial choices for the organization is attainable through meaningful communication of data and timely relevant information flowing through many channels (Mabert et al., 2003).

The critical project paths are communication, time, cost, strategy, pre-planning, and long-term business objectives considerations. These areas have their own set of risks which can foster or hinder the ERP system implementation. Still, pre-planning for mitigating such issues increases the success ratio, the author's study discovered.

The researchers concluded from the information collected on foundational considerations for enterprise resource planning and the impactful areas for success with ERP system installation. Note the human communication role throughout the integration process remains at the top of the list and relies on people for the overall project's favorable outcome (AboAbdo et al., 2019).

REFERENCES

Articles

AboAbdo, S., Aldhoiena, A., & Al-Amrib, H. (2019). Implementing Enterprise Resource Planning ERP system in a large construction company in KSA. Procedia Computer Science, 164, 463-470.

Allen, V. (2008). ERP security tools: data mining and analysis software can help auditors test access controls for key enterprise resource planning systems. Internal Auditor, 65(1), 25-27.

Anderson, M., Banker, R. D., Menon, N. M., & Romero, J. A. (2011). Implementing enterprise resource planning systems: organizational performance and the duration of the implementation. Information Technology and Management, 12(3), 197-212.

Akbulut, A. & Motwani, Y. (2005). The road to ERP success; understanding end-user perceptions. Journal of International Technology and Information Management, vol 14, issue 4, article 2. https://scholarworks.lib.csusb.edu/cgi/viewcontent.cgi?article=1153&context=jitim

Amazon (AWS). https://aws.amazon.com/opensearch-service/?sc_icampaign=pac_gc-600-alt_opensearch_freetier&sc_ichannel=ha&sc_icontent=awssm-10840_pac&sc_iplace=signin&trk=7c442aa1-6ae0-4b80-9897-6de067c8c7f0~ha_awssm-10840_pac

Beheshti, H. M., & Beheshti, C. M. (2010). Improving productivity and firm performance with enterprise resource planning. Enterprise Information Systems, 4(4), 445-472.

Caldwell, A. (2020, Oct 7). 4 key ERP implementation

strategies. https://www.netsuite.com/portal/resource/articles/erp/erp-implementation-strategies.shtml

Chofreh, A. G., Goni, F. A., & Klemes, J. J. (2018). Steps towards the implementation of sustainable enterprise resource planning systems. Chemical Engineering Transactions, 70, 283-288.

Cook, R. (2013, Aug 9). Communication in ERP. https://community.spiceworks.com/topic/2454742-communication-in-erp

Florida Tech, (2022). ERP functional areas. https://www.floridatechonline.com/blog/information-technology/erp-functional-areas/

Holy Bible, New International Version. (2011). www.zondervan.com

Jacobs, F. R., & Bendoly, E. (2003). Enterprise resource planning: developments and directions for operations management research. European Journal of Operational Research, 146(2), 233-240.

Jorgensen, P. Jeff. (1997). Amazon.com Shareholder Letter. www.amazon.com

Lefran, D. (2016, March 17). Why communication plays an essential role in BPM https://www.retailcustomerexperience.com/blogs/why-communication-plays-an-essential-role-in-bpm/

Mabert, V. A., Soni, A., & Venkataramanan, M. A. (2003). Enterprise resource planning: Managing the implementation process. European journal of operational research, 146(2), 302-314.

Miller, K. (2020, Mar 19). 5 critical steps in the change management process. https://online.hbs.edu/blog/post/change-management-process

Momoh, A., Roy, R., & Shehab, E. (2010). Challenges in enterprise resource planning implementation: State-of-the-art. Business Process Management Journal, 16(4), 537-565.

Motiwalla, L., & Thompson, J., (2012). Enterprise Systems for Management, second edition. www.pearson.com

Oliver, D., & Romm, C. (2002). Justifying enterprise resource planning adoption. Journal of Information Technology, 17(4), 199-213.

Panoroma consulting group, (2012, July 23). The importance of two-way communication during an ERP implementation. https://www.panorama-consulting.com/the-importance-of-two-way-communication-during-an-erp-implementation/

Panorama Consulting Group. (2021, Feb 1). https://www.panorama-consulting.com/erp-project-governance/

Perston, M. (2022, Jan 21). System development life cycle guide. CloudDefense. https://www.clouddefense.ai/blog/system-development-life-cycle

Potts, B. (2020, Feb 17). Six tips for creating an ERP communications plan. https://www.thirdstage-consulting.com/six-tips-for-creating-an-erp-communications-plan/

Prabhakaran, J. (2022, March 2). How to document your change management process. https://document360.com/blog/change-management-process/

Radack, S. (2009). The system development life cycle (SDLC). NIST. https://www.nist.gov/publications/system-development-life-cycle-sdlc

Stobierski, T. (2020, Jan 21). Organizational change management: what it is & why it's important. https://online.hbs.edu/blog/post/organizational-change-management

Stratman, J. K. (2007). Realizing benefits from enterprise resource planning: does strategic focus matter? Production and Operations Management, 16(2), 203-216.

TekStream. (). https://www.tekstream.com/services/amazon-web-services-aws/

Trexin, (2014, June 2). Key success factors for an ERP implementation. https://www.trexin.com/key-success-factors-for-an-erp-implementation/

Ultra-Consultants accessed (2022, May 27). 5 change management strategies for an ERP project. https://ultraconsultants.com/erp-software-blog/change-management-strategies-for-an-erp-project/

Wang, E. T., Lin, C. C. L., Jiang, J. J., & Klein, G. (2007). Improving enterprise resource planning (ERP) fit to organizational process through knowledge transfer. International journal of information management, 27(3), 200-212.

Wright, S., & Wright, A. M. (2002). Information system assurance for enterprise resource planning systems: Unique risk considerations. Journal of information systems, 16(s-1), 99-113.

❊ ❊ ❊

ACCOUNTING CODE

Topic 350: Intangibles – Goodwill and other internal use "Under the current guidance in Subtopic 350-20, Intangibles—Goodwill and Other—Goodwill, an entity is required to monitor and evaluate goodwill impairment triggering events throughout the fiscal year" (FASB, 2020, Dec 21) noted. https://asc.fasb.org/imageRoot/09/125982809.pdf

Topic 360: Property, Plant, and Equipment "also known as fixed assets. Fixed assets are grouped into four main categories as shown below: Land and land improvements, Buildings, Machinery and equipment, Furniture and fixtures" (AccountantTown, 2011) highlighted. https://www.accountanttown.com/fasb/assets/property-plant-and-equipment-2/

Topic 320: Investments – Debt and Equity Securities "included under the financial statement asset section and offers guidance on investment instruments that represent either a creditor relationship (debt) or an ownership interest (equity) and provides standards for reporting such investments according to generally accepted accounting principles" (Bartleby.com, 2021) noted. https://www.bartleby.com/essay/The-Fasb-Codification-Topic-320-Investments-Debt-FKZCKJ7WXG385#:~:text=The%20FASB%20Codification%20Topic%20320%3A%20Investments-Debt%20and%20Equity,accepted%20accounting%20principles%20%28GAAP%29%20%28FASB%20ASC%20320-10-05-2%2C%202016%29.

Topic 805: Business Combinations "Business acquisitions are

accounted for in accordance with FASB, requires the reporting entity to identify the acquirer, determine the acquisition date, recognize and measure the identifiable assets acquired, the liabilities assumed, any non-controlling interest in the acquired entity, recognize and measure goodwill or gain from the purchase" according to (SEC XML 95 R27.htm IDEA: XBRL DOCUMENT). https://www.sec.gov/Archives/edgar/data/865752/000110465915058216/R27.htm

Topic – 410: Asset retirement and environmental obligations. https://materialaccounting.com/article/asset-retirement-obligation-aro-accounting-asc-410/